Please visit our website, www.garethstevens.com. For a free color catalog of all our high-quality books, call toll free 1-800-542-2595 or fax 1-877-542-2596.

Cataloging-in-Publication Data

Names: Kennon, Caroline.
Title: September 11, 2001 / Caroline Kennon.
Description: New York : Gareth Stevens Publishing, 2019. | Series: History just before you were born | Includes glossary and index.
Identifiers: LCCN ISBN 9781538231357 (pbk.) | ISBN 9781538230305 (library bound) | ISBN 9781538233153 (6 pack)
Subjects: LCSH: September 11 Terrorist Attacks, 2001--Juvenile literature. | Terrorism--United States--Juvenile literature.
Classification: LCC HV6432.7 K47 2019 | DDC 973.931--dc23

First Edition

Published in 2019 by
Gareth Stevens Publishing
111 East 14th Street, Suite 349
New York, NY 10003

Copyright © 2019 Gareth Stevens Publishing

Designer: Sarah Liddell
Editor: Therese Shea

Photo credits: Cover, p. 1 James Devaney/Contributor/WireImage/Getty Images; newspaper text background used throughout EddieCloud/Shutterstock.com; newspaper shape used throughout AVS-Images/Shutterstock.com; newspaper texture used throughout Here/Shutterstock.com; halftone texture used throughout xpixel/Shutterstock.com; p. 5 Joseph Sohm/Shutterstock.com; p. 7 (main) MARK D. PHILLIPS/Staff/AFP/Getty Images; p. 7 (Yousef) MarioFinale/Wikimedia Commons; p. 9 (main) THOMAS COEX/Staff/AFP/Getty Images; p. 9 (bin Laden) MIR HAMID/DAILY DAWN/Contributor/Gamma-Rapho/Getty Images; p. 10 Agranome et Chofers/Wikimedia Commons; p. 11 U.S. Navy/Handout/Getty Images News/Getty Images; p. 13 MattWade/WikimediaCommons; p. 14 Mysid/Wikimedia Commons; p. 15 Debivort/Wikimedia Commons; p. 17 Victorgrigas/Wikimedia Commons; p. 19 Hiro Oshima/Contributor/WireImage/Getty Images; p. 21 (main) Brooks Kraft/Contributor/Corbis Historical/Getty Images; p. 21 (seal) Corkythehornetfan/Wikimedia Commons; p. 23 (NATO flag) railway fx/Shutterstock.com; p. 23 (main) USAF/Handout/Getty Images News/Getty Images; p. 25 (map) Electionworld/Wikimedia Commons; p. 25 (inset) JIM HOLLANDER/Staff/AFP/Getty Images; p. 27 (top) Francis Dean/Contributor/Corbis Historical/Getty Images; p. 27 (bottom) The White House/Handout/Getty Images News/Getty Images; p. 28 Gary Hershorn/Contributor/Corbis News/Getty Images.

Printed in the United States of America

CPSIA compliance information: Batch #CW19GS: For further information contact Gareth Stevens, New York, New York at 1-800-542-2595

CONTENTS

Words in the glossary appear in **bold** type
the first time they are used in the text.

ACTS OF TERROR

We hear the words "terrorism" and "terrorist" a lot on TV and the radio. Just like the root of the words—"terror"—suggests, terrorism is frightening. The term can be used to describe any violent acts committed by someone or a group of people for the purpose of achieving their demands. In the twenty-first century, however, terrorism is strongly associated with **militant** and **extremist** groups such as ISIS and al-Qaeda.

The attack on the World Trade Center in New York City by the terrorist group al-Qaeda on September 11, 2001, is probably the most famous modern example of terrorism in US history. On that day, not only did a small group of men kill thousands, but they also succeeded in frightening the entire world.

MORE TO THE STORY

In 2001, the risk that an American in the United States would be killed by terrorists was less than one in 100,000. In the 10 years that followed, that chance was one in 56 million. Americans became safer after the events of September 11, also called 9/11.

THE WORLD TRADE CENTER WAS A SYMBOL OF AMERICAN PROGRESS IN ONE OF THE MOST FAMOUS CITIES IN THE WORLD.

A CRIME DEFINED

Terrorism isn't just any crime committed by someone who hates another person or group. The US federal code says terrorism is "the unlawful use of force and violence against persons or property to intimidate [frighten] or coerce [pressure] a government, the civilian population, or any segment thereof, in furtherance of political or social objectives." This means that terrorism is a crime meant to threaten as well as communicate a certain political or social goal.

ENTER AL-QAEDA

The September 11 attacks weren't the first time terrorists attacked the United States, or even the World Trade Center. On February 26, 1993, a group of **Muslim** extremists exploded a bomb in the parking garage underneath the World Trade Center buildings, killing six people and injuring more than 1,000.

A phone number belonging to a man named Osama bin Laden was discovered on a list of calls made by the plotters of the bombing. Bin Laden, a Wahhabi Muslim, founded the militant Islamic organization called al-Qaeda in the late 1980s. Bin Laden and his followers believed the Western influence of countries such as the United States hurt the religion of Islam. Al-Qaeda wanted to not only harm the United States but also remove all of its influence from the Middle East and ideally the world.

MORE TO THE STORY

The more than one billion Muslims in the world follow different branches of teaching. Some strict Wahhabi Muslims believe all who aren't Wahhabi are enemies. Most other kinds of Muslims are open to the beliefs of others.

"YES, I AM A TERRORIST"

Ramzi Yousef was the chief planner of the 1993 bombing. He chose the World Trade Center as his target. These "Twin Towers" were the second tallest buildings in the world at the time. Yousef was captured. Before he was sentenced, he said, "Yes, I am a terrorist and proud of it as long as it is against the US government." He called the government "liars and butchers." Yousef was placed in solitary confinement at a federal prison in Colorado.

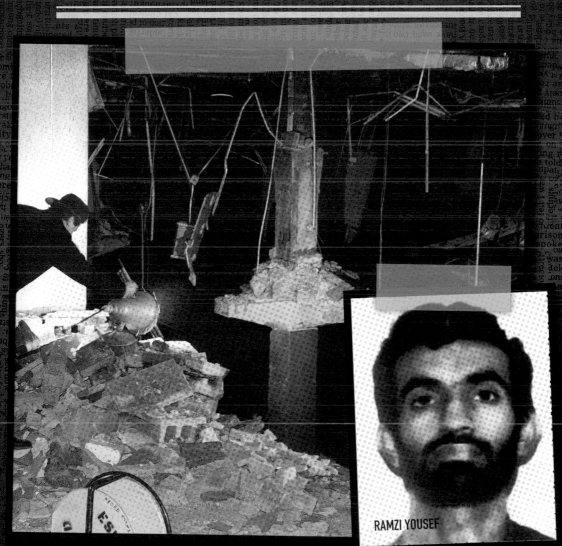

RAMZI YOUSEF

RAMZI YOUSEF WAS THE ORGANIZER OF THE FIRST WORLD TRADE CENTER BOMBING. HIS UNCLE WOULD LATER HELP PLOT THE 9/11 ATTACKS.

OSAMA BIN LADEN

In August 1996, bin Laden declared a holy war, or a war undertaken in the name of a religion, on the United States. But at that time, the United States was distracted by other threatening figures, such as Iraq's then-president Saddam Hussein. In February 1998, bin Laden and his associates issued a fatwa, or command, which claimed Muslims had a duty to kill Americans. He stated, "It is the duty of Muslims to prepare as much force as possible to terrorize the enemies of God."

In 1998, the FBI (Federal Bureau of Investigation), CIA (Central Intelligence Agency), and other agencies began to recognize the real danger of al-Qaeda when two American **embassies** were bombed in Africa. The United States accused bin Laden, among others, of planning these acts of terrorism.

MORE TO THE STORY

Osama bin Laden was born in Saudi Arabia to a very wealthy family. He was the 17th of 52 children and inherited great wealth when his father died.

OSAMA BIN LADEN

BOMBING AT THE AMERICAN EMBASSY IN KENYA

A TRUCK BOMB CAUSED A HUGE EXPLOSION AT THE US EMBASSY IN NAIROBI, KENYA, ON AUGUST 7, 1998. MINUTES LATER, A SIMILAR BOMB EXPLODED IN DAR ES SALAAM, TANZANIA.

OPERATION INFINITE REACH

In August 1998, US President Bill Clinton ordered **missile** attacks in Afghanistan against Osama bin Laden and al-Qaeda as part of Operation Infinite Reach. US intelligence had learned that bin Laden would be at a military camp at a certain time and planned to kill him. Of the attacks, Clinton said, "Let our actions today send this message loud and clear . . . We will defend our people, our interests, and our values." However, bin Laden escaped harm.

THE PLAN FORMS

The CIA's Counterterrorism Center (CTC) suspected bin Laden was planning a large-scale terrorist attack—and they were right. In the years leading up to 9/11, bin Laden asked four Muslim militants to sacrifice themselves in an attack against the United States. Mohammed Atta of Egypt was chosen by bin Laden as the leader of the group.

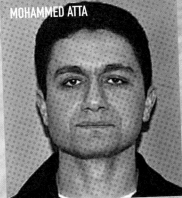

MOHAMMED ATTA

In 1999, the men learned they would be pilots in the so-called "Planes Operation." They would use American planes to attack the United States. Other terrorists would aid the pilots in taking control of the planes. There was no need to smuggle bombs onto the planes, and there was no need to come up with a complicated escape plan. The terrorists themselves were the weapons, and there would be no escape.

MORE TO THE STORY

Planning and executing the September 11 attacks is thought to have cost about $500,000.

THE TIMELINE

Osama bin Laden met with the 9/11 terrorists in late 1999. In March 2000, Mohammed Atta applied to flight schools in Florida for "a small group of young men from different Arab countries." By July 2001, Atta was told that bin Laden was anxious to put the plan into action because so many enemy agents in the country would eventually draw the attention of the US government.

MOHAMMED ATTA (RIGHT) IS PICTURED PASSING THROUGH AIRPORT SECURITY ON SEPTEMBER 11, 2001.

SEPTEMBER 11, 2001

On September 11, 2001, Mohammed Atta boarded American Airlines Flight 11, which departed Boston, Massachusetts, for Los Angeles, California, at 7:59 a.m. The plane had two pilots, nine flight attendants, and 81 passengers—including five terrorists. Because the pilots stopped communicating with air traffic controllers, it's thought that the plane was hijacked, or taken control of, within 15 minutes of takeoff. At 8:19 a.m., a flight attendant made an emergency call reporting that someone aboard had been stabbed. At 8:46 a.m., the plane flew into the north tower of the World Trade Center.

An 8:15 a.m. flight—United Airlines Flight 175—out of Boston to Los Angeles carried nine crew and 56 passengers, including five terrorists. This flight was hijacked at knifepoint. At 9:03 a.m., the plane hit the south tower of the World Trade Center.

MORE TO THE STORY

There were no survivors on either plane that hit the World Trade Center.

THE 9/11 ATTACKS HAPPENED ON A CLEAR FALL DAY, JUST AS MANY NEW YORKERS WERE GETTING TO WORK. AS OF AUGUST 2017, ONLY 60 PERCENT, OR 1,641, OF THE 2,753 WORLD TRADE CENTER VICTIMS' REMAINS HAVE BEEN IDENTIFIED.

THE TOWERS FALL

Even though it was second to be hit, the south tower fell first. The north tower didn't collapse until a half hour later. People who worked in the building rushed to get out. It's believed that about 200 people fell or jumped from the towers. When the north tower fell, the chief of the New York Fire Department, the superintendent of the Port Authority Police Department, and many other emergency workers were killed.

Besides the planes flown into the World Trade Center on September 11, two other planes were hijacked that morning. American Airlines Flight 77 left Washington, DC, at 8:20 a.m. with two pilots, four flight attendants, and 58 passengers on board, including five hijackers. At 9:37 a.m., the plane crashed into the Pentagon, the headquarters of the Department of Defense, killing everyone on the plane instantly.

CRASH SITE OF FLIGHT 93

At 8:42 a.m., United Airlines Flight 93 left Newark, New Jersey, for San Francisco, California, carrying a crew of seven, 33 passengers, and four terrorists. At 9:23 a.m., the pilots received a warning about the other hijacked planes. Minutes later, the terrorists entered the cockpit. Air traffic controllers believe they heard a struggle. The plane would crash-land in a Pennsylvania field about a half hour later.

MORE TO THE STORY

Some passengers aboard Flight 93 called their loved ones to say goodbye and let them know they planned on fighting back.

PENNSYLVANIA HEROES

When the pilots and passengers on Flight 93 realized what was happening, they took their fate into their own hands by forcing the plane to crash in an empty field in Shanksville, Pennsylvania. Everyone on board was killed, but this undoubtedly saved hundreds of additional lives. It's suspected the terrorists may have planned on flying into the Capitol, the White House, or perhaps even a nuclear power plant.

THE DAMAGE TO THE PENTAGON WASN'T AS SEVERE AS THAT AT THE WORLD TRADE CENTER. IT WAS REBUILT WITHIN A YEAR.

CHAOS IN NYC

When the towers of the World Trade Center fell, clouds of smoke and rubble from the buildings filled the streets. Many buildings surrounding the towers were damaged or fell as well. The fires that resulted in the collapses continued to smoke for more than 3 months after the attack. It was difficult to get away from the site of the attack and difficult to get close enough to help.

Nearly 3,000 people were killed that morning: about 2,750 in New York City (which included more than 400 police officers and firefighters who had responded to the scene); 184 people at the Pentagon in Washington, DC; 40 people in Pennsylvania; and the 19 terrorists who put the attack in motion.

MORE TO THE STORY

President Bush's response to the attacks raised his approval ratings from 55 to 90 percent after September 11—the highest approval rating for a US president ever recorded.

HUNDREDS OF POLICE AND FIREFIGHTERS RESPONDED TO THE SITE OF THE ATTACKS.

WORD REACHES THE PRESIDENT

At the time of the September 11 attacks, George W. Bush was president. He had been visiting a second-grade classroom in Florida when the planes hit. His chief of staff, Andrew Card, whispered into his ear that America was under attack. That night, President Bush gave a speech from the Oval Office in the White House, saying: "We will make no distinction between the terrorists who committed these acts and those who harbor them."

AFTERMATH

New York City is one of the most famous cities in the world. The World Trade Center had been a symbol of the city and American economic power in general. Hundreds of thousands of people were eyewitnesses to the towering buildings' destruction. Millions more watched the attacks and the aftermath live on television. It was a tragedy that was previously thought impossible. The United States had seemed almost **invincible** up to that point.

Not only were the city, country, and world shaken emotionally by the attacks, but there was also great financial damage because of the closing of the stock market and the cost of rebuilding. Additionally, tens of thousands of people were stranded in airports because planes were grounded throughout the country until September 13.

MORE TO THE STORY

It took 3.1 million hours of work and $750 million to clean up the 1.8 million tons (1.6 mt) of debris from the collapse of the World Trade Center. Cleanup was completed on May 30, 2002.

TELEVISED TERROR

The attacks on the World Trade Center happened in a place that gets widespread television coverage around the world. This was **strategic** for Osama bin Laden and al-Qaeda. The entire world was made aware that the United States had weaknesses and that al-Qaeda was dangerous and far reaching. Millions had seen what these terrorists were capable of with their own eyes. Al-Qaeda quickly went from being almost unknown to a household name—and a household fear.

THE UNITED STATES WAS THOUGHT BY MANY TO BE UNTOUCHABLE BEFORE 9/11.

DEPARTMENT OF HOMELAND SECURITY

The September 11 attacks changed the way the United States faced the issue of terrorism. To many, 9/11 showed how unprepared the country had been, even though more than 100 government agencies had responsibilities regarding national security before then. President Bush proposed a new department that would specialize in these tasks and in protecting the country against future threats. The Department of Homeland Security officially opened in March 2003. Its mission included fighting terrorism and aiding recovery after disasters.

The department was divided into four basic divisions: border and transportation security; emergency readiness; science and **technology**; and information analysis and **infrastructure** protection. The seal designed for the department includes images of land, sea, and air to show that all three areas would be guarded from harm.

MORE TO THE STORY

The Department of Homeland Security employs more than 240,000 people.

TOM RIDGE (CENTER) IS SWORN IN AS THE FIRST SECRETARY OF HOMELAND SECURITY. HE REMAINED IN THE POST UNTIL 2005.

THE SEPTEMBER 11TH VICTIM COMPENSATION FUND

The September 11th Victim **Compensation** Fund was set up from 2001 to 2003 to aid those affected by the attacks. The fund received 7,408 applications for the death or injury of loved ones. Of those applications, 5,560 people were given part of over $7 billion. The money given ranged from $500 to $8.6 million per person or family. The fund was reopened in January 2011 to continue to help people suffering after the attacks.

NATO

The rest of the world rallied to support the United States. Many countries reached out in sympathy, holding candlelight ceremonies to show unity against terrorism. On September 12, the French newspaper *Le Monde* ran the headline "Nous sommes tous Américains"—we are all Americans.

The United States and other governments were sure al-Qaeda was responsible for the attacks. For the first time ever, the North Atlantic Treaty Organization (NATO) acted on its Article 5, which meant its members would respond together to an attack on a member nation. NATO knew al-Qaeda was based in Afghanistan, but the **Taliban**-led government refused to hand over bin Laden or stop al-Qaeda activity there. On October 7, 2001, the United States and its NATO **allies** attacked Afghanistan.

MORE TO THE STORY

In addition to the NATO bombing campaign, planes dropped supplies to help Afghan citizens affected by the war.

NATO'S FLAG INCLUDES A CIRCLE THAT REPRESENTS UNITY AND THE COLOR BLUE TO SYMBOLIZE THE ATLANTIC OCEAN.

NATO BEGAN THE ATTACK AGAINST AFGHANISTAN WITH A BOMBING CAMPAIGN.

ALLIANCE OF NATIONS

NATO is an alliance between several countries, and it exists for situations like September 11. Its members agree that an attack against one member is an attack against all. The United States, France, and the United Kingdom are among the founding members, and 26 other countries in North America and Europe are also members. Four years after the end of World War II, the treaty NATO is based on was signed on April 4, 1949.

THE WAR IN AFGHANISTAN

Within months of the United States and its allies invading Afghanistan, thousands of enemies were killed or captured. Many al-Qaeda leaders went into hiding while the American government tracked down its members across the world.

The United States destroyed the al-Qaeda base in Afghanistan, so the September 11 attacks can be seen as a failure for al-Qaeda. One of al-Qaeda's leaders, Saif al-Adel, tried to argue that the attacks were a way to provoke the United States into reacting and making foolish mistakes, but al-Qaeda didn't seem prepared for the ground invasion that followed the bombing. Members fled their training camps in preparation for air strikes, fell to NATO forces, and were never able to recover the power they once held in Afghanistan.

MORE TO THE STORY

The United States still has troops in Afghanistan as of 2018, making the war the longest in US history.

THE PATRIOT ACT

Shortly after Afghanistan was invaded, President George W. Bush signed the USA PATRIOT Act into law. Like the creation of the Department of Homeland Security, this was an attempt to strengthen American security. Not everyone agreed with it, however, because it gave law enforcement the ability to search homes and personal records of citizens without permission. In 2015, President Barack Obama signed the USA Freedom Act into law, which limited the government's authority to collect data.

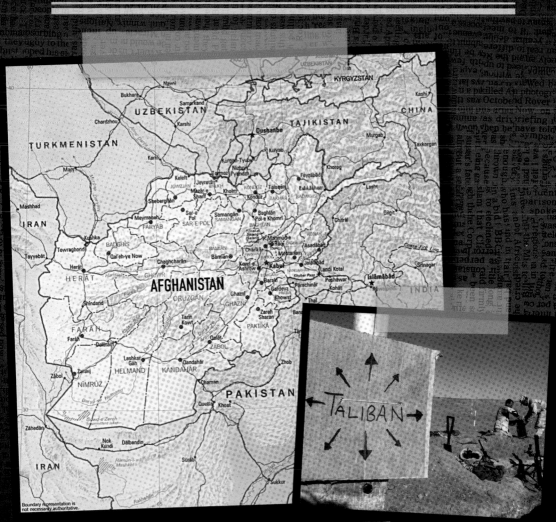

THE WAR IN AFGHANISTAN OVERTHREW THE EXTREMIST TALIBAN GOVERNMENT.

FINDING BIN LADEN

It wasn't enough that al-Qaeda's base was destroyed—the United States wanted the man behind the attacks. The government needed to send the message that terrorism wouldn't be accepted. Bin Laden, however, was hard to locate. President Bush issued a $25 million reward for any information leading to his death or capture. A video surfaced in December 2001 proving that bin Laden had helped plan the attacks and was pleased about the destruction of the towers. He called the people killed "the enemy."

Nine years after the attacks, President Barack Obama was informed by US intelligence that bin Laden was living in Pakistan. On May 2, 2011, a small team of US Navy SEALs successfully attacked bin Laden's base and killed him.

MORE TO THE STORY

Osama bin Laden was buried in the Arabian Sea within 24 hours of his death, according to Islamic law.

OSAMA BIN LADEN WAS KILLED IN 2011 IN THE CITY OF ABBOTTABAD IN PAKISTAN.

THE MISSION TO KILL OSAMA BIN LADEN WAS RECORDED BY CAMERAS CARRIED BY NAVY SEALS. VICE PRESIDENT JOSEPH BIDEN (LEFT), PRESIDENT OBAMA (SECOND FROM LEFT), AND SECRETARY OF STATE HILLARY CLINTON (SECOND FROM RIGHT) WATCHED FROM THE WHITE HOUSE.

A SAFER PLACE

After bin Laden was killed, President Obama remarked: "The cause of securing our country is not complete. But tonight, we are once again reminded that America can do whatever we set our mind to. That is the story of our history, whether it's the pursuit of **prosperity** for our people, or the struggle for equality for all our citizens; our commitment to stand up for our values abroad, and our sacrifices to make the world a safer place."

STRONGER TOGETHER

The events of 9/11 permanently changed life in the United States and in the world. Words like "terrorism" and "extremism" became part of our everyday language. Traveling by plane became a much more serious security matter. Fear increased all over. And unfortunately, American Muslims became the target of suspicion and hate crimes.

ONE WORLD TRADE CENTER

The aim of al-Qaeda, Osama bin Laden, and their terrorist acts were to make people afraid—to hold power over a powerful country. Since September 11, the United States has made great efforts to honor the nearly 3,000 people killed that day and to show that this country cannot be so easily terrorized. We learned that day that no one is invincible, but as a country, we can overcome **adversity**.

MORE TO THE STORY

One World Trade Center was built where the Twin Towers once stood. Nearby, the September 11 Memorial honors those killed on 9/11 and in the 1993 World Trade Center bombing.

FIGHTING ISLAMOPHOBIA

The terrorists responsible for September 11 were Muslim extremists. This has led many frightened Americans to fear the religion of Islam and people of the Middle East. In 2000, 28 anti-Islamic hate crimes were committed in the United States. In 2001, that number jumped to 481. It's important to remember that a person's religion or skin color doesn't identify them and that extremists are a small group, not a majority, of Muslims.

TIMELINE OF SEPTEMBER 11, 2001

1996: OSAMA BIN LADEN OFFICIALLY DECLARES HOLY WAR ON THE UNITED STATES IN AUGUST.

1998: BIN LADEN ISSUES A FATWA AGAINST AMERICANS IN FEBRUARY.

2000: MOHAMMED ATTA OF EGYPT APPLIES TO FLIGHT SCHOOLS IN FLORIDA.

2001: ATTA IS TOLD BY AN AGENT OF BIN LADEN IN JULY TO PUT THE "PLANES OPERATION" INTO ACTION.

SEPTEMBER 11, 2001:

8:46 A.M.: AMERICAN AIRLINES FLIGHT 11 HITS THE NORTH TOWER OF THE WORLD TRADE CENTER IN NEW YORK CITY.

9:03 A.M.: UNITED AIRLINES FLIGHT 175 HITS THE SOUTH TOWER OF THE WORLD TRADE CENTER.

9:37 A.M.: AMERICAN AIRLINES FLIGHT 77 HITS THE PENTAGON IN WASHINGTON, DC.

9:59 A.M.: THE SOUTH TOWER OF THE WORLD TRADE CENTER COLLAPSES.

10:03 A.M.: UNITED AIRLINES FLIGHT 93 CRASHES IN A FIELD OUTSIDE OF SHANKSVILLE, PENNSYLVANIA.

10:28 A.M.: THE NORTH TOWER OF THE WORLD TRADE CENTER COLLAPSES.

2001: THE UNITED STATES AND ITS NATO ALLIES BEGIN AN ATTACK ON AFGHANISTAN ON OCTOBER 7.

2001: A VIDEO IS RELEASED ON DECEMBER 13 IN WHICH OSAMA BIN LADEN TAKES RESPONSIBILITY FOR THE 9/11 ATTACKS.

2003: THE DEPARTMENT OF HOMELAND SECURITY OFFICIALLY OPENS IN MARCH.

2011: OSAMA BIN LADEN IS KILLED BY A SMALL TEAM OF NAVY SEALS IN PAKISTAN ON MAY 2.

GLOSSARY

adversity: a state of serious or continued difficulty or misfortune

ally: one of two or more people or groups who work together

compensation: payment for something done or suffered

embassy: the offices of an official agent of a country called an ambassador

extremist: one who believes in and supports ideas that are very far from what most people consider correct or reasonable

infrastructure: the system of public works of a country, state, or region

invincible: incapable of being conquered or overcome

militant: a person who will use force to support a cause or beliefs

missile: a rocket used to strike something at a distance

Muslim: a follower of the religion of Islam

prosperity: the condition of being successful or thriving

strategic: having to do with the use of a clever plan or skill

Taliban: an extremist Islamic armed force in Afghanistan

technology: the practical application of specialized knowledge. Also, tools, machines, or ways to do things that use the latest discoveries to fix problems or meet needs

FOR MORE INFORMATION

BOOKS

Benoit, Peter. *September 11 Then and Now.* New York, NY: Children's Press, 2012.

Brown, Don. *America Is Under Attack: September 11, 2001: The Day the Towers Fell.* New York, NY: Square Fish/Roaring Brook Press, 2014.

Doeden, Matt. *Impact: The Story of the September 11 Terrorist Attacks.* North Mankato, MN: Capstone Press, 2016.

WEBSITES

9/11 Memorial & Museum
www.911memorial.org/
Here is the official website of the September 11 Memorial.

September 11th
www.brainpop.com/socialstudies/ushistory/september11th/
This website features a movie about what happened on September 11, 2001.

INDEX